Blue Banana Ltd. Partnership

555 QUOTES AGAINST WOMEN

(With Particular Reference to Wives)

Federico Riva

PUBLISHED IN 2009 BY BLUE BANANA LTD. PARTNERSHIP
Blue Banana Limited Partnership
Sen Jan Lane, Nanai Road, Patong, Kathu, Phuket, Thailand.

info@quotes-book.com
www.quotes-book.com

ISBN: 6-11902450-6

ISBN-13: 978-611-90245-0-2

Designed by Marlon Goulart da Silveira
Cover Photograph: @ Fotolia
Portrait of Federico Riva by Iko Haat
Copy editing: Alessio Giacomucci

TABLE OF CONTENTS

ACKNOWLEDGEMENTS

I'd like to thank all my friends and family for their support; in geographical order (from West to East): Alessio *"Al"* Giacomucci (from Philadelphia, U.S.A), Carlos "*Carlo*" Brito (from New York City, U.S.A.), Luca *"Zollo"* Zollino (from Madrid, Spain), Jack *"Papa Jack"* Higgs (from Birmingham, England), Davide *"Cicciuz"* Cerruto (from Monza, Italy), Elena *Mamma* Cazzaniga Riva (from my heart), Jacopo *"Jac"* Gonzales (from Rome, Italy), Fabio Montuori (from Avezzano, Italy), Antonio *"Anto"* Riva (from Monza, Italy), Ugo *"Ughetto"* Salem (from Rome, Italy), Chanphen *"Teerak"* Yingchungam (from Buriram, Thailand), Barney *"Abomination"* Tscherewik (from Phuket, Thailand), Clinton *"Clint"* Robinson (from High Wycombe, Australia), and all the women I've ever met in my life, who inadvertently gave me great support with their constant, sincere and unintentional inspiration.

Phuket Island, September 2009.

~ VIII ~

To my next wife

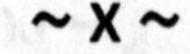

INTRODUCTION & INSTRUCTIONS FOR USE

In the pages that follow you will find 555 quotes dedicated to women.

I use the term 'quotes' and not 'aphorisms' in an attempt to attract people into buying (or stealing) this book, making them believe it is a collection of famous quotes, when in actual fact they are all original aphorisms that I have created and written myself.

The best way to read these quotes is to follow suit in the way that I wrote them: slowly, with an immense love for women, abstractedly and in places that are most suited for mulling over concepts: in bed, in the car and (for men) in the bathroom.

The choice of number 555 is arbitrary, and has nothing to do with the kabala, which I know very little about, even less than what I know about women.

And I know nothing at all about women.

~ XII ~

WOMEN

1.   Women love more, care more and lie better.

2.   Man invented the wheel. Soon after, woman invented the sharp curve.

3.   If you find a woman who always does what you want, you must want something wrong.

4.   Don't beat your woman. Most like it.

5.   If you think women are bad at driving, you've never asked a woman for directions.

6.   There are two kinds of women: before and after.

7.   *Career men* bring their work home; *career women* bring it even into bedrooms.

8.   A prawn's heart is in its head. A woman's heart is in ours.

9.   A woman is like the law; the more you know about it, the less you respect it.

10.   Elegant women always know their rightful place. After stealing it from some- one else.

11.   Women take years to learn how to drive, and a few seconds to learn how to hitch a ride.

12.   One kind of red rose fits hun- dreds of kinds of women.

13. If you can't stand a woman who lies, you have probably not dealt with a woman who doesn't.

14. Recent studies have shown that men who don't ask questions have more sincere wives.

15. *Pessimist*: someone who thinks that women are all the same.
Optimist: someone who thinks that women are all the same.

16. There are two types of women to avoid: those who don't know what you like and those who know exactly what you like.

17. I know I am communicating well with a woman when I agree with what I say.

18. On vacation, I always have problems with my computer, because I insisted on taking my wife with us.

19. Seducing an honest woman is like stealing from a house with the front door open. It takes a lot of courage.

20. Finding the right woman is like finding a needle in a haystack: difficult, painstaking and useless.

21. When I read that, every 12 seconds, a man beats a woman in the USA, I was really shocked. By their precision.

22. Women arrive late not because they do not respect you, but because they hate time; and I fully understand that, look at what time does to them.

23. Open and honest communication is important for a good relationship, but crucial for a bad one.

24.   There are two things worth living for: one makes you fat, the other is always on a diet.

25.   Human beings are divided into men and women. Women are divided into human and non-human beings.

26.   Women, like cats, have 9 lives; but cats have them one after another.

27.   I'm not angry if my wife speaks to others. I'm angry if she speaks to me.

28.   Women have fewer rights than men, but they use them all.

29.   A man spends half his life looking for the perfect woman and the other half making believe he found her.

30. It is not true when they say women aren't what they used to be. They are, but they are all over 90 years of age now.

31. Never beat your wife; because if you then stop beating her, she'll know you got another woman.

32. Working women are paid less than working men, but non-working women are paid much more than non-working men.

33. It is not true that female doctors are less competent. It's just that their patients are sicker.

34. You can say you know the female sex when, looking at two completely different women, you can't find a single difference.

35. Women are quite violent people: they throw things and keep the house.

36. And behind every ex-successful man there's a great ex-wife.

~ -7- ~

CELIBACY

37.   If you have no one waiting for you at home, you'll never get home late.

38.   When you're single you complain there's nothing good on TV. When you're married, you complain there's nothing interesting after you have turned it off.

39.   When you make love to your wife you are making love to your ex-girlfriend.

40.   The last time I agreed with my wife was when we decided where we would go on our honeymoon; she wasn't even my wife then.

41.   A bachelor is a single man. A married man is a single man with a wife.

42.   Some say that it's bad luck to get married on a Tuesday. But any day is a good day to remain a bachelor.

43.   Why do you want to remain a bachelor? Get a mortgage!

44.   What was so great the first time I met my wife? Well, she wasn't my wife yet.

45.   A bachelor should always learn how to make his own dinner. In case he gets married.

46.   The opposite of a hysterical wife is a calm celibacy.

47.   A *bachelor* is someone who enjoys sex outside marriage; a *married man* is someone who enjoys sex outside the home.

48.   New brides shouldn't worry. Married men don't go fishing more than bachelors; they just lie more.

49.   *Engagement*: Attempted marriage, punishable by wife.

WEDDINGS

50.   100% of weddings end in marriage.

51.   The wedding is a waste of money. That's why women love it.

52.   It would have been sufficient if I'd chosen my wife with half the care she took to choose my wedding suit.

53.   30 minutes before my wedding, it started to rain; it's never stopped since.

54.   *Marriage*: the thing that comes after the wedding. Very after, if lucky.

55.   Women remember the day of the wedding. Men, all the days before.

56.   Staying sober during your wedding is much easier than staying sober during your marriage.

57.   When did I meet my wife? Shortly after our wedding.

58.   My wife planned our wedding for 7 months and her marriage for 20 years.

59.   I also cried at my wedding, but 2 years later.

60.   After some years of marriage, your wedding won't look that expensive anymore.

61.   The wedding day: 50% are people you don't know and 50% are people who don't know you.

MARRIAGE

62.   Clever men, like stupid men, end up getting married; but only stupid men are proud of it.

63.   What makes a marriage successful? Common interests and different bathrooms.

64.   Mutual incomprehension is the cause of 50% of all divorces and 100% of all marriages.

65.   I am against marriage after sex.

66.   The right age to get married? The Middle Ages, maybe.

67. Marriage is simple arithmetic: 1 + 1 will always equal 2.

68. I married at 25 and divorced at 35. I wasted the worst years of my life because of her.

69. If, after a few years of marriage, you are in bed with your wife and you feel cold, don't get a new blanket; get a new wife.

70. You don't need to get married to despise women, but it can be of help to despise yourself.

71. After a quarrel, a well-adjusted married couple goes back to the way they were before. This is the problem.

72. *Woman on top* is a wife's favorite position. But not in sex, in marriage.

73.   I believe in a happy marriage the way I believe in God. I'm pretty sure it's out there, but I've never seen one so far.

74.   *A true love* happens only once or twice in a life time. After that, you can get married.

75.   Marriage is teamwork: 2 teams.

76.   *Marriage* is not just two people living in the same space and sharing meals together. That is a *happy marriage.*

77.   Marriage, like voting, is democratic. You don't count at all, but you get *the right to complain.*

78.   I prefer cohabitation to marriage; but marriage is fine too, when cohabitation is avoided.

79. I got married at 30, my wife was 28. After 1 year, we were a 60 year old couple.

80. Today, I saw a book entitled: "*How to save your marriage*". I didn't buy it immediately.

81. If you cannot defeat your enemy, befriend him. If you don't succeed in be-friending him, make him at least wash the dishes.

82. Marriage is not the best way to prove to a woman you love her; it's just the last.

83. Have I ever thought of getting mar-ried? Yes, very carefully. That's why I didn't.

84. Children cannot get married be-cause the law considers them too young to be punished.

85. Marriage gives you the chance to do what you didn't do before the wedding; for example, to reflect.

86. The recipe for a good marriage is to never write it down on paper.

87. Between two evils, always choose the one who is already married.

88. Marriage is like a bar brawl; it can be amusing thinking about it, 10 years later.

89. If you aren't happy, marry a good girl. You won't be happy either, but at least you'll know why.

90. An *expert in women* is someone who knows nothing about marriage.

91. *To be or not to be?* Just don't get married.

92.   Ask a happy, married man about his marriage. You'll learn nothing about happy marriages, but a lot about lying.

93.   A happy marriage is just a matter of respect: you must lose a bit of yours.

94.   Marriage? Never say never. Just say: *No, thanks.*

95.   99% of geniuses are married. That shows that genius has little to do with wisdom.

96.   I'll never forgive my wife for marrying me.

97.   Why did I get married? I was happy with her and I overreacted.

-V-

WIVES

98.   My wife loves me with all my heart.

99.   Before you cheat on your wife, think about it 10 times. Then, do it.

100.   Husband and wife have identical rights: both have the right to a lawyer.

101.   For a wife, *freedom* is not going wherever her husband wants.

102.   After some years, at best, your wife turns into your sister. At worst, *you* turn into her sister.

103. Behind every great man there is a secretary who reminds him of his wife's birthday.

104. My wife never lies to me; she lies to herself, and then tells me the truth.

105. To desire a girl who could be your daughter is immoral; to desire a woman who could be your wife is just stupid.

106. Words cannot be unsaid, so be careful in what you say to your wife when you're angry. And very careful, when you're happy.

107. The secret for a successful marriage? Exactly: secrets.

108. When my wife goes to the bathroom she does so for one reason only: to get some privacy. Hers or mine.

109. Don't complain if your wife snores during sleep. Mine snores during sex.

110. My wife has always been nasty. As a child she was so nasty, that the dark was afraid of her.

111. The difference between a wife and a stranger? A wife takes time to become one.

112. If you don't know how to make your wife happy, you won't know how to hurt her either.

113. Marriages often fail. Wives, seldom do.

114. All fiancées want to know where you were last night. But wives want to know where you *really* were.

115. My wife told me she dreamt of her death last night. Now I understand why the same night I dreamt of winning the lottery.

116. If your wife lies to you, it's alright. If she lies to other guys too, you should start to worry.

117. When I saw my wife for the first time, I realized she was the woman of her dreams.

118. You can easily know what an angry wife thinks of you, but not what a sweet one does.

119. A Muslim is someone who doesn't need to get three divorces to have four wives.

120. All of Henry VIII's wives were related to each other. No wonder at all. Apparently, it goes for all wives.

121.   I was happily married for 6 years; the first year, thanks to my wife and the other 5, despite her.

122.   After 20 years, I can say that, with my wife, it's just like the day before we met for the very first time.

123.   She was a good wife, for a woman.

124.   *Rape* is a hate crime. *Marriage* is a love crime.

125.   Don't beat your wife. Beat mine.

-VI-
HUSBANDS

126. Getting married isn't natural at all. Nobody, as a kid, wants to become a husband.

127. 20% of married men die in their own home, while only 2% manage to actually live in it.

128. An erect stance distinguishes human beings from all animals and most husbands.

129. For a happy marriage, a man should be taller, older, richer and sadder than his wife.

130. A good husband shouldn't batter his wife. And a good wife shouldn't call the police.

131. Every day, thousands of husbands kill their wives during sleep; then they wake up and go to work.

132. It's not true that all husbands are misogynists. A misogynist hates all women, a husband just his own.

133. A woman can desire to be a man, but she will hardly desire to be her own husband.

134. A husband who believes in eternal love? A naïve pessimist.

135. Never ask a man why he got married. Either he won't like your question or he won't like his answer.

136. Getting married means switching from a single life to a double life.

137. I am an immature person; my wife is still deciding what I will do when I'm grown up.

138. I've never wanted to be a painter, or a husband: never join a profession where you'll be much more considered after death.

139. A woman who speaks little proves the intelligence of her husband.

140. Sure, women love cats more than husbands. Have you ever seen a reward poster for a husband?

141. A good husband knows something about good plumbing. As a good plumber knows something about good wives.

142. How to define someone who carefully chooses a good lawyer before divorcing? Wise, after the event.

143.   He married at 28, still very young, without even leaving a note.

SEX

144. The most common sexual problem in men is not getting an erection. It's using it.

145. The only precaution I take before having sex is to make sure she's a woman.

146. A few minutes before sexual intercourse, a man's brain can shrink by 50%.

147. Just petting is not that bad; if you are a dog.

148. You need to do two things to make a woman happy: make love to her and make her laugh. Preferably not at the same time.

149.   Men can interrupt a love story if the sex is not satisfying. Women can interrupt an intercourse if love is not satisfying.

150.   At 50, the most common sexual fantasy in women is to have sex.

151.   Love is a pretext: men use it to have sex; women use it to avoid having sex.

152.   I have always been a careful guy. I always buy a girl when I go out with a packet of condoms.

153.   Sex is different from love: in sex, experience counts.

154. Women should know that the area of the brain responsible for sexual attraction in men is in a different location than in women. Actually, it's quite far from the brain.

155. The real sexual issue is not that women can simulate orgasm, but that men cannot dissimulate erections.

156. The G-spot is an invention by women to force men to keep trying to find it.

157. The *fair sex*? It's when the price is fair too.

158. The most hideous form of violence is the refusal of sex to a consenting adult.

159. The best aphrodisiac is time; 2, 3 weeks without getting laid.

160. I like simplicity in women: a drop of perfume, a brush of mascara and a half hour.

161. Sex and love are not two different things; they are just two different women.

162. Women can fake orgasms, but men can still fake sleeping.

163. Sex is a strange activity: first we learn to have it on our own, and then end up asking others for help.

164. Sex is important in a good relationship. Essential, in a bad one.

165. I don't care about being present at the birth. I would be happy enough to be present during conception.

166. Sex is very important in love, but in friendship it is much more likely.

167. Sex with a condom? I have tried it, but I still prefer having it with a woman.

168. Women cannot love two men at the same time. But, then again, they're quite good in doing so in the same space.

169. Old women hide their possessions under the mattress, young women on top.

170. *Heterosexuality*: doing unto others what you wouldn't like others to do unto you.

171. Scientists have proved that the more orgasms you have, the older you get. Apparently, either my wife lies about her age or about her orgasms.

172. What is the difference between love and sex? Safe sex exists.

173. Only women can easily tell the difference between sex and love: sex hurts in the beginnings, love in the endings.

174. I agree with anal sex and I agree with marriage. As soon as we are clear on whose marriage we are talking about.

175. Women should accept that nothing stays the same size forever. That's true for sex and for love.

176. Penis size doesn't matter; unless you're a woman.

177. A woman spends 1/3 of her life on a mattress. A beautiful woman on many more than one.

178. In men, a kiss stimulates 29 muscles and paralyzes one brain.

179. The strangest place where I made love? My wife.

180. Women can have 3 types of orgasm: vaginal, clitoral and fake. And the fake orgasm is divided into vaginal and clitoral.

181. A couple is in tune when it doesn't need a good reason not to have sex.

182. It is time to divorce when your wife makes more noise sleeping than when she's making love.

183. Sex education is a pretty simple matter. Before going to bed with a girl, you should say: *may I?*

184. Pigs' orgasm lasts 30 minutes. And sows don't bother too much about foreplay.

185. Sex is the only activity where a woman can strike for weeks without ever having worked one day.

186. I don't discriminate about sex. I discriminate about gender. And within the right gender, any sex is fine.

187. Husbands usually sleep shortly after having sex. Wives, shortly before.

188. The difference between love and sex? When she pants, it's *sex*. When she yells, it's *love*.

189. The difference between sex and love is that in the first case you quickly realize if you are doing it alone.

190. If you get sex for free, it is only because someone, somewhere, has already paid for you.

191. Flings are fine if you go on vacation. But with women it is better to book.

192. It is not true that, for men, sex is the most important thing in the world. It is just the most important thing in a woman.

193. The favorite sex position for wives is: *man on top,* and husband at the office.

194. Women are the only animals that, for pleasure, don't have sex.

195. A man with a great woman behind him has just misread the Kamasutra.

196. Sex is the friction of opposites.

197. Porn movies show muscled men having sex with women. Romantic movies show skinny men trying.

-VIII-

CHEATING

198. If it is true that women are unfaithful in their hearts, I can safely say that I have met many women with big hearts.

199. My wife has always been the suspicious type. When she had our first child she took a paternity test to make sure I was the real father.

200. Women will betray you first with their imagination, then in their heart, then with their body and then more or less with anybody.

201. It took me years to manage to forgive my wife for cheating on her first husband.

202. My wife would never cheat on me with another man. She always cheats on me with the same one.

203. When a romance is over, fools turn to their friends for comfort; a wise man turns to his wife.

204. Before deciding to have a relationship with a woman, I always insist on meeting her husband.

205. Attack is not the best form of defense; lying is.

206. Cheating doesn't ruin marriages. Cheating *helps* marriages; it's discovering cheating that does it.

207. Bigamy is forbidden by law, only because monogamy is already forbidden by nature.

208. Take note of the woman you marry, because you will base the choice of your lover accordingly.

209. Should cheaters pay more in the divorce? Yes, much more attention.

210. Testing how much your wife loves you is as wise as testing your blood sugar: you will only be in for an unpleasant surprise.

211. If she knows where your erogenous zones are, she's your lover; if she knows where your socks are, she's your wife.

212. There are essentially 2 kinds of women: *cheaters* (who cheat on you) and *good cheaters* (who don't).

213. Learning to trust your wife is switching from thinking that she doesn't cheat on you to not thinking she's cheating on you.

~ ~ ~

214. Women feel a strong urge to get married after they turn 30; nobody wants an affair with a mature woman, if she's not married.

215. The secret of my happy marriage? I don't know. My lover knows the answer, but she has never told me.

216. Women fake orgasms. Men fake traffic jams.

217. The first time a man catches his wife cheating on him, he shouldn't over-react. It's hardly the first time.

218. Cheating on a wife does not necessarily end in divorce. So, try something different.

219. After 2 years of marriage therapy, my wife finally stopped cheating on me, and started cheating on her lover.

220. If your husband suddenly stops having sex with you, maybe he is cheating on you. If your husband stops gradually, then that's alright.

221. If your wife starts acting strangely, chances are she's cheating on you; or he's cheating on her.

222. 20% of married women have extramarital affairs. The remaining 80% have marital affairs.

223. For women sex is not that important. Actually, they can cheat on you in many different ways.

224. I'm all for marriage. If you are lucky, you'll have great sex with your wife. If you're not, you'll have it with the wives of others.

225. After a few years of marriage you'll have a relationship with another woman; whether your mistress or your wife.

226. You can cheat on your wife and be a bad husband or be a good one, cheating on yourself.

227. Once a cheater, always a cheater. In the end, we are very reliable.

228. Trust is not essential to a happy marriage. Trust is essential to a happy affair.

PROFESSIONALS

229. Whores are not all the same either.

230. Giving money to a woman you don't know is prostitution. Giving money to the florist you know is romance.

231. All women hate the rain: whores because they work less; wives, because they work more.

232. Considering the age of some of the women on the street, I can confirm that prostitution is the oldest job in the world.

233. Prostitutes simulate orgasms; wives, the opposite.

234.   To say that all women are whores, it would be necessary to have met all the whores.

235.   *Whore* has about twenty exact synonyms and not one exact antonym.

236.   Men go to prostitutes for special jobs wives normally don't do. Listening, for example.

237.   I have nothing against prostitution; sometimes against the prices.

238.   On the other hand, not all whores are women.

239.   Poor men go to prostitutes. *Vice versa* for rich men.

240.   I don't think all women are whores because I've had bad experiences with them. Just the contrary.

241. To insult a lady, offer her money in exchange of sex. To really piss her off, offer her little money.

242. A prostitute is a woman who doesn't need to say she's proud of you in order to get to your wallet.

243. If a woman makes love for 20 dollars, it's women exploitation. But for 1,000 dollars it seems more like men exploitation.

244. From a woman who doesn't sell her body, you cannot expect a dime in discount.

245. You pay a whore to get laid. With your wife it's just the opposite.

246. Paying a woman is an inelegant way to show a woman you like her, since it's the cheapest.

247. Prostitution and marriage are crimes; the first is organized, the second is not.

248. There are 80,000 prostitutes in Los Angeles alone. Well, they're not so alone...

249. A whore makes 10 men happy every day, instead of making one unhappy his entire life.

250. Women are like taxes: paying them is unpleasant; not paying them is risky.

251. Good women don't think prostitution is immoral, just unfair.

252. If you think all women are for sale, you're wrong; and you're an optimist.

253. I'm a romantic guy; I always pay.

254. Why pay for sex? Just marry a nice girl, and you will have sex anytime she wants.

255. I've been hooked up with prostitutes a couple of thousand times, but I didn't like it.

256. If you pay to have sex, it's *prostitution.* If you work to have sex, it's *marriage.*

257. A bad girl enjoys her life, a good one enjoys yours.

258. What is the difference between a whore who weighs 110 lbs and a decent woman who weighs 130 lbs?

-X-

LOVE

259. It takes one to be alone. To feel alone, it takes two.

260. I've experienced sex without love; it's much better than sex without women.

261. When you have an orgasm, it's *sex*; when she has an orgasm, it's *love*.

262. My wife showed me her love by making food for me. I showed her my love by eating it.

263. If *true love* is giving without expecting anything in return, well, I would say that true love exists.

264. *Maturity* means realizing that, in the end, false love exists.

265. Love is the attrition of opposites.

266. The true loves of my life? Very few; I can count them on the fingers of one punch.

267. It's not true you need to say to a woman that you love her only to get her into bed. You need to say it to 5 women, to get only one into bed.

268. You can fall in love only twice in a lifetime: when you desire her and when you remember her.

269. It takes time to get to know another person and, when you finally do, you discover that it was indeed another person.

270.   Growing means shifting from asking if she loves you to asking what does *love* mean.

271.   You can really love just two, three times in your whole life. But you can say *I really love you* as many times as you want.

272.   The painful parts of a love story? Knees and elbows.

273.   Poets find names for feelings; women, surnames.

274.   The difference between sex and love? If you have been married for a few years, none.

275.   How to define a couple where he loves himself and she loves herself? A couple in love.

276.   Actually, you don't need to know someone's habits to love him. You need it to rob him.

277.   Loving is a matter of experience. The less you have, the more you'll love.

278.   Babies and love stories are always born with blue eyes.

279.   I love women, with a lot of imagination.

280.   You cannot forget your first love. And for sure you can't remember it right.

281.   Don't miss the good old days. Those are what the current days come from.

282.   You can talk to yourself. But it takes two to remain in silence.

HOUSE & HOME

283.   There are two things that benefit from competition between men: women and home gardens.

284.   A woman feels at home when she has difficulty getting to the door.

285.   Getting married and setting up a home means having a place to get away from, every morning.

286.   You can either be at home or feel at home. Not both.

287.   It's very impolite to say to a married man: *make yourself at home.*

288. A few months after I got married, I found a stranger in my house who didn't want to get out.

289. All that a man needs to be happy is this: a well looked after garden, a woman in the house and a quiet dog. Or any mixture of the three.

290. My wife, one day, slammed the door and stayed.

-XII-

MONEY

291.   Sex is like money. If it's dirty, you enjoy it better.

292.   *Size* is for sex what *money* is for love: it doesn't matter, if you have it.

293.   Giving women money as a present is risky: they don't all have the same size.

294.   Behind every great man, there is a great woman. Who is waiting.

295.   There are two categories of women: those who want to marry a rich man, and those who have married a rich man.

296. Only two types of people enter a store with no intention of spending one dollar: robbers and women. Robbers speak less and are more courteous.

297. It isn't true women care only about money; between two multi-millionaires, a woman will always choose the kinder one.

298. When a woman says *yes* it may mean *no*; when she says *no* it may mean *yes*; but if she says 100 dollars, it means exactly 100 dollars.

299. You should never marry a woman richer than you, or not as rich as you.

300. Rich men are surrounded by false women. Poor men, by poor women.

301. There are two types of women, those who do it because of money and those who, because of money, don't do it.

302. American women are simple, some even say gullible. Tell them you are a multi-millionaire and they desire you on your word.

303. If you think that 50% of women are just interested in money, well, you have a pretty limited vision.

304. Thinking that poets get lots of women is like thinking that mathematicians make a lot of money.

305. The difference between a rich man and a romantic man is that the former doesn't need to act like the latter.

306. My wife would follow me to the ends of the earth, if she needed some money.

307. Why get married? Just gather 100 people you don't really like, and buy them dinner.

308.   A woman is considered to be economically independent when her husband is rich enough.

309.   My wife's lucky number is 0; many of them.

310.   You rarely see a pretty woman eating alone at the restaurant. Who eats alone, normally pays the bill.

311.   And who, being married, is rich?

312.   A wife won't ever interfere with her husband's job, as long as she can interfere with his salary.

313.   There are 10 main reasons why a marriage fails: the first refers to financial problems; the other 9 are irrelevant.

314. My wife left me unexpectedly, leaving me with just a little note. 5 dollars, if I remember well.

315. 50% of all women are only interested in money. The remaining 50% preferred not to answer.

316. Don't pay for sex; many women can mistake it for love.

-XIII-

THE FEMALE MIND

317. Women don't even believe weighing scales; how can you imagine they believe men?

318. Blondes are stupid, but fake blondes are not fake stupid.

319. Every man has a feminine side. The same doesn't go for every woman.

320. Judging women is hard, only because there's nothing to compare them with.

321. There are two types of lies women can stand: the lies they say and the compliments they receive.

322. Feminists say that *there is no female mind.* Well, I must agree.

323. Women have a different level of intelligence compared to men: useful for winning a game of chess, but not enough to play it.

324. Clever women don't think that all men are untrustworthy idiots. In fact, they think they're trustworthy idiots.

325. Uneducated and stupid women think that blacks are better at sex. Educated and intelligent women think they're better at jazz.

326. Personal computers are the clear demonstration that anything with a good memory does not get on well with women.

327. Women are more independent than men. They don't need others to be unhappy.

328. Women can be angry; men can be angry too. Women can be happy; men can be happy too. But only women can be angry and happy at the same time.

329. Women: they want to be understood, but not too much.

330. Normally, loving a woman means nothing more than trying to stick to our first impression.

331. Men distinguish themselves from animals and women because they are able to recognize their own image in the mirror.

332. The difference is not that women are unfaithful in their minds, but that they are unfaithful with intelligence.

333. Recent studies have shown that women are less susceptible to pain; that of others.

334. I'm not sure about the *female mind*. But the *female body* yes, that's quite more practical.

335. The intelligence of women is emotional. Instead of relying on their brains, they rely on the emotions of men.

336. There are two moments when a marriage can be said to be happy. When we think our friends' marriage is, or when our friends think ours is.

337. Men invent cures; women, diseases.

338. A woman's intelligence is not different from that of a man; her stupidity is.

339. 90% of geniuses are men. The other 10% just look like.

340. A recent study has showed that women are much more intelligent than men; but it was wrong.

341. Women are much better at multi-tasking than men; they can say they love you, and think they don't, while they actually do.

-XIV-
WOMEN'S
BEHAVIOR

342. For women, loving is like fainting. For 1 woman who really faints, 1,000 feel they're fainting. But they don't.

343. Don't exploit women. They want to do it on their own.

344. Two men become friends when they have something in common. Two women, when they have someone in common.

345. A woman normally doesn't respect her husband because she finds it hard to envy him.

346.   The man who thinks that women often cry for no reason is simply an idiot.

347.   When my wife is wrong, she tries, and tries, and tries again until she finds someone who says she's right.

348.   Women don't have all the same taste for men. I do agree; some taste better.

349.   Women fight for what they believe in. And against anybody else who believes the same.

350.   There are two types of animals: those who don't speak, called beasts; and those who don't listen, called women.

351.   An *intellectual* makes an impression on a beautiful woman by using difficult words. A beautiful woman, by not understanding them.

352. I don't like sincere women. Sincere women fart in front of you.

353. For men, the main reason for car accidents is drinking. For women, it's driving.

354. Women don't need a good reason to cry; they just need a good couch.

355. Women's suffrage has slightly bettered the conditions of women and seriously damaged politics.

356. Woman is the only animal that is able to not-smile.

357. Help a woman. She won't forget it. And when she needs help again, she will turn to you once more.

358. You can't understand women; you can't understand men either. But with men you can have a conversation.

359. Women always keep their promises. The ones they made to themselves.

360. You'll never see a woman crying alone.

361. For men, jealousy is a way of being; for women, of having.

362. Women's last name changes after marriage. And it is usually the thing that changes least.

363. Men lie as often as women. It's just that men know it's wrong.

-XV-

FOOD

&

BEVERAGE

364. A woman must learn how to cook before her wedding day; a man, just after it.

365. After drinking too much, your hearing is less sharp, but your wife's yelling is louder.

366. My wedding took place in a restaurant; as well as my marriage.

367. Whether of cheeseburgers or girls, you can never trust a picture.

368. Buy a large refrigerator; this is where you will be preserving your marriage.

369. Women don't like eating alone because they have nobody to talk about.

370. The best diet for a woman is the one that makes her best girlfriend fatter.

371. I don't say dirty words to my wife to liven up our sex. I do it to liven up my food.

372. Yes, I'm unfaithful to my wife in my mind. Sometimes it happens that, while eating hers, I think of other soups.

373. My wife: when angry, she doesn't cook for me; when very angry, she does.

374. With my wife I never discuss sensitive subjects during dinner: like food, for example.

375. Men are more inventive at cooking. But women are much more inventive at non-cooking.

376. Choosing your wife according to how a woman cooks is like choosing a restaurant according to how the cook makes love.

377. If you think that women are like cats, remember that cats don't cook.

378. Alcohol plays a role in 50 percent of all arrests for marital abuse. I've always known: cops shouldn't drink on duty.

379. Getting to know a woman's soul is like getting to know the recipe of a dish. It doesn't change the taste of it.

380. There are only two types of wives: those who don't cook for you and those who are calling you for dinner.

381. I certainly prefer a woman who fakes orgasms to a woman who fakes cooking.

382. Give a man a fish and he'll eat one day. Give a woman a fish and she'll yell at you a week.

383. *Marriage is tricky;* you start having hot sex in the kitchen and after a few years you end up eating cold food in bed.

384. My wife dreamed of my death last night. But she wasn't sleeping, she was cooking.

385. My wife insisted that I quit drinking; because, when I drink, I'm happy.

386.   It's not that women cook worse, as they age. It's just that their husbands get more sincere.

387.   Getting married is going from eating when you're hungry to eating when supper is ready.

388.   Never enter a restaurant or a woman that doesn't list prices on the menu.

389.   Marriage is like a new recipe. Before you try it, you don't know how good it is. And after, it's too late.

390.   Getting married because you're in love is like buying a restaurant because you're hungry.

391.   A wife is a woman who knows what food you don't like, and cooks it for you.

392. Drinking must really be unhealthy; every time I'm drunk, my wife starts crying.

393. When I have a heated discussion with my friends, the best way my wife has of defending me is to say I'm drunk.

394. Don't mix alcohol with medicines or women.

395. Alcohol causes about 20% of all divorces and about 40% of all marriages.

396. Recently, I started drinking at home with my wife. When I am totally drunk, I go out and beat up my bartender.

-XVI-

FAMILY

&

FRIENDSHIP

397.   As a matter of fact, your wife is just your mother-in-law's daughter.

398.   I asked my fiancée to introduce me to her parents, but they didn't like me. So, I asked her to introduce me to some others.

399.   If you spend money on a woman you can get her into bed; if you spend a lot more you can even get to meet her parents.

400. The only infallible method of male contraception is saying: *I don't know this woman.*

401. When you get married, you kill 1 mother and give birth to 2 mothers-in-law.

402. Marriage is a compromise: between what your wife wants and what your mother-in-law doesn't.

403. Before getting married, don't look at her mother to see how your wife will look when she gets old; look at the father to see how *you* will look.

404. Lending money to friends is risky; to women it's just impossible.

405. According to the Catholic Church, a man can have only one wife but an endless number of brothers-in-law.

406. Remember that only your mother can really love you. And not after you turn 10.

407. Before choosing a woman to marry, observe her mother closely. If she is still alive, don't marry her.

408. There's only one mom. And you cannot change her.

409. Friendship can be put to the test every day. Love, only once.

410. Sex without condoms can produce an undesired child. Love without condoms, many more than one.

411. Sure, I'm against marriage: marriage is sex that involves children.

412. My girlfriend got a pregnancy test this morning: the result says I'm an idiot.

413. When a woman loves her husband, she loves him like a mother loves a child. Someone else's child.

414. *Maternal feelings* are easily found in every woman who hasn't had children yet.

415. I didn't get married and I don't have children. I'm trying to give my parents a good example.

416. Friends don't let friends get divorced. They keep on lying.

417. *Marriage* is a soul, two bodies, and parents on Sundays.

418. A woman will always give her best friend her best advice; the best for herself.

419.   I would never go to bed with the wife of one of my friends. Every man has to take care of these problems on his own.

420.   Friendship between a man and a woman is not impossible. Between a woman and a woman it is.

421.   I certainly have nothing against marriage. Many of my dearest friends are married.

422.   A true friend is someone who meets a woman who would be the perfect wife for you, but doesn't introduce her to you.

423.   A diamond is forever; give one to your mother.

XVII

BODY & BEAUTY

424. I don't want a woman like Barbie; Barbie speaks too much.

425. If you have a very beautiful wife, you don't need anything else, and anyway you can't afford it.

426. If you want to embarrass a beautiful woman, don't ask her how old she is, but what she does for a living.

427. The blonde is always blonder on the other side of the fence.

428. My wife takes much better care of her nails than of me. And her nails are dead.

429. Up close, there are few women who are really beautiful. Closer still, there are few that are really ugly.

430. Women spend their youth convinced they are ugly and their old age convinced they are still beautiful.

431. Sure I know where the erogenous zones of my wife are. They're at home right now.

432. Ugly women make people wait for hours, before nobody rings the bell to take them out to dinner.

433. Sure women can change. Look at a pretty woman, then wait 20 years and look at her again. And you will see how much they can change.

434. If you love beautiful women, you must love crowded places too.

435. There are two ways of really appreciating a beautiful woman: close-up, (in space) and from afar (in time).

436. A woman's heart beats faster than men's. And it stops faster too.

437. Every woman prefers to vaguely resemble a beautiful actress than to be identical to a pretty woman.

438. Soon after death, a man's body rapidly gets cold, while his wife rapidly gets hot.

439. Two kinds of people are obsessed with their weight. Women and boxers. Women don't wear gloves.

440. The truth is in the middle. At least for women. Anatomically speaking.

441. What is the second thing a man notices in a woman with big breasts?

442. A woman without makeup, with dirty hair and with untidy nails doesn't feel at ease going out, but she's ok staying at home. With you.

XVIII

CLOTHES & SHOES

443.   My wife told me to choose: *either cigarettes or me.* In the end she accepted a new dress.

444.   Before buying a dress, a woman always checks it in the dark.

445.   I don't care too much how a woman gets dressed, as long as she does it in silence.

446.   It is not easy to imagine being in a woman's shoes; one never has a nice pair to wear.

447.   Men must be very gross people. The fact that they don't really like a suit is enough for them to not buy it.

448.   A *wife* is a woman who, before going to bed, gets dressed.

449.   Keep in mind that mature women live in the past, but they still buy clothes in the present.

450.   It is quite hard judging a woman by her clothes; every day, you change your mind.

451.   The first time my wife got undressed before me, she was ashamed. Last time she got undressed, *I* was.

452.   *Transvestite*: a man who dresses like a woman. *Husband*: a man who dresses like his woman wants.

453.   My wife has more dresses than Maria Callas, she doesn't know how to sing, and she is still alive.

454. Lies have long legs and high heels.

~ - 85 - ~

455. How should a man dress for his wedding? Slowly, very slowly.

HOMOSEXUALS

456. I have nothing against same-sex marriages. I'm not in favor of same-marriage sex though.

457. The fact that a man is married doesn't mean he's not gay, it just means he's not happy.

458. Women are all the same. Men are all the same. Only homosexuals seem slightly different to me.

459. It's impolite to ask a woman *his* age.

460. When I meet a man of 50 who is still a bachelor and has no children, I don't suspect he's gay. I suspect he's smart.

461.   A *straight man* is someone who cannot really see the external beauty of a man and the internal ugliness of a woman.

462.   When a man is 'different', it means he's gay; when a woman is 'different', it means she's good.

463.   A *feminist* is a woman who wants lesbians to have the same rights as gays.

464.   I don't like gays. That's why I'm in favor of gay marriage.

-XX-

FEMINISM

&

CHAUVINISM

465. A *feminist* is a woman who enjoys being cursed at, even when she's not in bed.

466. A *feminist* is a woman who would like ugly women to have the same privileges as beautiful ones.

467. A *male chauvinist* is someone who thinks women are inferior to men, but superior to what they actually are.

468. A *misogynous man* is someone who thinks he despises women more than even they do.

469. A *misogynist* is a man who loves women, but also knows them.

~ - ~

470. A *feminist* is someone who can't explain why, during a shipwreck, women have to be saved first.

471. A *female misogynist* is a woman who has understood that other women are just like her.

472. If women are not all the same, why should they have the same rights?

-XXI-
METAPHORS
&
LANGUAGES

473.   The most spoken tongue in the world is the female one.

474.   Love is like a rose; if it's fake, it smells less, but lasts longer.

475.   Marriage is like Chinese communism; it's a nice idea, as long as you don't live there.

476.   A woman is a mammal with 2 heads, 100 hands and 400 pairs of shoes.

477. Understand women? There is nothing to understand. Women are natural, like the rain, like the sun. Well, perhaps more like the rain.

478. Women are like insects: they are annoying, or poisonous; or you can only see them on TV.

479. If the adjective of *man* is *human,* what is the adjective of *woman?*

480. Since women are like cats, I strongly suggest you marry a cat.

481. A *career man* is a man engaged in business; a *career woman* is a woman engaged to a career man.

482. Love is watching her sleep. *Marriage* is hearing her sleep.

483. Women are like cats. But you can have 5 cats in your house.

484. Women are like paintings. When they are priceless it just means they cost way too much.

485. A husband is somebody who doesn't have sex, always with the same woman.

486. You can be a great lover without knowing how to love; as you can speak French perfectly, without ever having been to Paris.

487. Hanging out with foreign women is always an advantage: you learn a language quickly and get to know a woman slowly.

488.   Getting to know a woman is like learning Japanese; you'll take 20 years, and still you cannot say you can really speak Japanese.

489.   Women, like cats, have 9 lives. If married, 10.

490.   *Love, to*: transitory verb.

491.   Women are like cats. But live much longer.

492.   Woman is a noun; unless you use it to call a man, and then it turns into an insult.

-XXII-

DIVORCE

493. Women arrive late at weddings. Men, at divorces.

494. My wife found me with another woman, and to get back at me, she did not file for a divorce.

495. The law protects women after divorce and men before marriage.

496. The law states that a wife, after a divorce, must be provided with the same standard of living that caused the divorce.

497. Marriage is a compromise: between what your wife was like before the wedding and what she will become after filing for divorce.

498. If you've never been divorced you can already hate women, but not lawyers yet.

499. Marriages, like divorces, are rarely consensual.

500. There is only one thing more tragic than when your wife asks for a divorce: it's when your mistress asks for one.

501. The main difference between marriage and divorce is that, in the second case, the relatives celebrate in separate restaurants.

502. *Knowledge is power*, unless you speak about marriage, in which case it is divorce.

503. Divorce is not the dissolution of marriage. Normally, it happens to be the solution.

504. The bright side of being fired is that your wife will file for divorce shortly after.

505. The fact that a woman is a bit stupid is not enough to file for divorce, but it's always a good reason to get married to her.

506. Getting divorced is easier than getting married; in divorces, you don't have to choose who.

507. Divorced women live in poverty. Divorced men work in poverty.

508. Alimony: money paid by a husband to his wife following a divorce; before a divorce, it is called love.

DISEASE

509.   *Nymphomania*: a psychiatric matter; unless you're a man, and then it's just a matter of luck.

510.   The only real risk of unsafe sex is not having it.

511.   For a woman, premature ejaculation is anytime a man reaches an orgasm before buying dinner.

512.   *Rigor mortis*: muscular rigidity occurring a bit too late.

513.   Hitler got married the very last day of his life. This shows he was mentally ill, but not stupid.

514. Erectile dysfunction torments 12% of all men; erectile function torments the remaining 88%.

515. Women are much more fragile than men; they suffer from depression, while men just stick to heart attacks.

516. *Women's heart disease* is more often diagnosed in men.

517. 30% of wives are medically depressed. The remaining 70% simply miss their moms.

518. Marriage is not a medicine at all; it just tastes like one.

519. If one person talks alone, he needs a psychiatrist. If two persons talk alone, they need a lawyer.

520. The only remedy for snoring is sleeping alone.

521. Anytime I see my wife, it feels like the first time I saw her. And the first time I saw her, I was sick.

522. 1% of adult males die of a heart attack while having sexual intercourse; 99% trying to have one.

523. Deafness torments 10% of all adult men and consoles 100% of all adult husbands.

524. Menopause is the third cause of depression in women. The first in men.

525. Sex is chemistry. Marriage is meds.

526.   Women don't suffer from premenstrual syndrome. Women have premenstrual syndrome. Men suffer from that.

527.   *Psychiatric treatment of battered women.* Wasn't battering the treatment?

-XXIV-

DEATH

528. I hate it when my wife snores: it means she is still alive.

529. Man shoots his wife dead before taking his own life, back.

530. I'm against marriage; I'm also against fire arms, but I can't say I am against the combination of the two.

531. Only death should dissolve marriage! Romans 7:2-3. Apparently, they didn't specify *natural* death.

532. If your wife doesn't believe that you won't get married after her death, the best thing to do is prove it to her.

533.   Women kill less, but hurt more.

534.   I'd like my wife to be like Greta Garbo: classy, elegant, dead.

535.   I have always had a relationship based on understanding and mutual trust with my wife. We agreed that, when I die, I can have another woman.

536.   I told my wife that I wanted to kill myself. She asked me: *When?*

537.   Men are 6 times more likely to be killed by lightning than women and 60 times more likely to be killed by women than by lightning.

538.   Wives are divided into three categories: alive, dead, and on the phone.

539. If you kill your wife you'll be judged by 12 people who don't know you, instead of by 1 person you don't know.

540. My wife is very generous; she donates her organs to unknown people, and she's still alive.

541. A man shot his wife dead. The victim was 44, his wife was 36.

542. The difference between a widower and a divorcé? A widower had more patience.

543. I've always wanted to be a successful man: to be remembered by posterity after my death, and by my wife, before.

544. When you argue with your wife, remember that words can kill. But shotguns kill better.

545. There are two kinds of animals who have an incredible memory: elephants and women. Killing elephants is now considered immoral throughout the world.

546. If a man kills his wife, it's *uxoricide*; if somebody else does it, it's just luck.

547. If you keep thinking about killing your wife, you don't need a shrink; you need a plan.

548. I've never thought of killing my wife. But, now and then, I think about her suicide.

549. *Widower:* someone who is certain there is life after death.

550. Women live long because they love arriving late for a date.

551. Don't kill your wife. If you enjoy it, you can't do it again.

~

552. There are two things that are impossible to carry off: a perfect murder and a perfect marriage; but in the first case, you can count on some help from your lawyer.

553. *Uxoricide*: a divorcé who trusted guns more than lawyers.

554. *Man killed his wife by strangulation.* Why? He was old school.

555. When I am dead, I want my wife to be cremated.

Keyword Index

The following numeration refers to the aphorism number and not to the page.

www.ingramcontent.com/pod-product-compliance
Lightning Source LLC
LaVergne TN
LVHW041320200726
843509LV00009B/561